# ROMANIA



By Jagger Youssef and
Laura L. Sullivan

EXPLORING WORLD CULTURES

Cavendish Square

Published in 2027 by Cavendish Square Publishing, LLC
2544 Clinton Street, Buffalo, NY 14224



Second Edition



Website: cavendishsq.com



Cataloging-in-Publication Data

Names: Youssef, Jagger. | Sullivan, Laura L.
Title: Romania / Jagger Youssef and Laura L. Sullivan.
Description: Second edition. | Buffalo, NY : Cavendish Square Publishing, 2027. | Series: Exploring world cultures | Includes glossary and index.
Identifiers: ISBN 9781502677044 (pbk.) | ISBN 9781502677051 (library bound) | ISBN 9781502677068 (ebook)
Subjects: LCSH: Romania--Juvenile literature.
Classification: LCC DR205.Y68 2027 | DDC 949.8--dc23

Writers: Jagger Youssef; Laura L. Sullivan (second edition)
Editor: Therese Shea
Designer: Deanna Lepovich

The photographs in this book are used by permission and through the courtesy of: Cover ChrisChips/Shutterstock.com; pp. 4, 13 trabantos/Shutterstock.com; p. 5 Sarfaraz82/Shutterstock.com; p. 6 CristianMihart/Shutterstock.com; pp. 7, 27 (top) Gaspar Janos/Shutterstock.com; p. 9 (top) Mihai/Wikimedia Commons; p. 9 (bottom) Revolutia Bucuresti 1989 000/Wikimedia Commons; p. 10 Constantin Grigorita/Shutterstock.com; p. 11 MAVRITSINA IRINA/Shutterstock.com; p. 12 Vectorcarrot/Shutterstock.com; p. 15 (top) bdavid32/Shutterstock.com; p. 15 (bottom) Wirestock Creators/Shutterstock.com; p. 16 Iryna Dzvonkovska/Shutterstock.com; p. 17 Solar Studio/Shutterstock.com; p. 18 BearFotos/Shutterstock.com; p. 19 Economica20/Shutterstock.com; p. 20 Creativitate25/Shutterstock.com; p. 21 Emily Marie Wilson/Shutterstock.com; p. 22 Adriana Iacob/Shutterstock.com; p. 23 Oana08/Shutterstock.com; p. 24 Cristian-Alexandru/Shutterstock.com; p. 25 Roberto Sorin/Shutterstock.com; p. 27 (bottom) Dan POTOR/Shutterstock.com; p. 28 Victor Moussa/Shutterstock.com; p. 29 Dragos Asaftei/Shutterstock.com.



CPSIA compliance information: Batch #CS27CSQ: For further information contact Cavendish Square Publishing LLC at 1-877-980-4450.

Printed in United States of America

# CONTENTS

# INTRODUCTION

Romania is a country in southeastern Europe. It is known for its beautiful **landscape** and interesting past. Romanians are connected to many other peoples and histories of Europe. It was once part of the Roman Empire. Then it was ruled by the Ottoman Empire. Its people lived under **communist** rule for a time too. Finally, Romania became an independent, or free, democratic country in 1989. This means Romanians elect, or choose, their country's leaders.

*Bucharest is Romania's capital and oldest city.*

Today, Romania is a country with a successful, growing **economy**. Its people are proud of their nation's natural beauty, including the Carpathian Mountains, Danube **Delta**, and Lake Vidraru. Their history is preserved in many old buildings, including castles. Romanians can also boast of tasty foods, good music, and fun activities. More people around the world are visiting Romania every year and appreciating the rich **cultures** of this nation.

***Romania is the twelfth largest country in Europe. It is about 92,000 square miles (238,300 square kilometers).***

# GEOGRAPHY

Romania is surrounded by many other countries. Ukraine lies to the north. Bulgaria lies to the south. Hungary is west of Romania, while Serbia is southwest. Moldova lies to the northeast. Romania also borders the Black Sea on the southeast. The Danube River flows along Romania's southern border. The Danube is the second-longest river in Europe. It meets the Black Sea.

*The Danube River begins in Germany and ends in Romania, where it flows into the Black Sea.*

Romania has many hills and mountains. The Carpathian Mountains are in the center of the country. Moldoveanu Peak is the tallest. It is 8,346 feet (2,544 meters) high. Romania has plateaus too. These are sometimes called tablelands because they are high, flat, rocky areas that look a bit like tables.

*The Carpathian Mountains run through eight countries.*

**FACT!**
The Carpathian Mountains stretch about 900 miles (1,448 kilometers) in all.

## WHAT'S THE WEATHER LIKE?

Romania has a temperate climate. This means that it is not too hot in the summer or too cold in the winter. However, the weather is colder in the mountains.

# HISTORY

In ancient times, Romania was called Dacia. The Romans took control of what is now Romania in 106 CE. Many different peoples **invaded**, however. Later, Turkish people called the Ottomans took over. They ruled from the 1400s to the 1800s. Romania became independent in 1878. A monarchy, or rule by a king or queen, was set up in 1881. It lasted until World War II (1939–1945).

During the war, Romania's **prime minister** joined sides with Germany, Italy, and Japan. In 1944, King Michael had the prime minister removed and switched sides in the war. Romania then helped England, France, the United States, and the Soviet Union win. However, the Soviet Union took over Romania after. Romania was a communist country until a **revolution** in 1989. Romania then set up a democratic government.

**FACT!**

Romania elected its first president, Ion Iliescu, in 1990.

King Michael I (1921–2017) was the last king of Romania.

## HISTORY IN ITS NAME

The name Romania comes from the Latin language. It means "citizen of Rome." However, it didn't take on this name until 1862.

Over 1,000 people died in the Romanian revolution, which overthrew the communist government.

# GOVERNMENT

Romania adopted a constitution, or set of laws, in 1991. It set up a government with three branches: executive, legislative, and judicial. The president, prime minister, and Council of Ministers make up the executive branch. The president is elected by the people and leads the country. The president chooses the prime minister who runs the government.

*Nicușor Dan became president of Romania in May 2025. Presidents serve five-year terms.*

*The legislative branch of Romania's government meets at a building called the Palace of Parliament.*

**FACT!**
All Romanian citizens 18 and over can vote in elections.

The Romanian parliament is the legislative, or lawmaking, branch of the government. There are two groups within it, the Chamber of Deputies and the Senate. Members of these groups serve four-year terms.

The judicial branch is made up of courts. The highest court in the country is a Supreme Court of Justice. Judges serve six-year terms.

## LOCAL GOVERNMENTS

Romania has 41 counties and the city of Bucharest, which each has a local government. Mayors and councils deal with local issues.

# THE ECONOMY

Romania has a strong and fast-growing economy. The country is a member of the European Union (EU). This group, or union, of nations makes it easy for people, money, and goods to move between the different member countries. Romania's economy is one of the fastest-growing in the EU. Romania mostly trades with other countries in the EU, especially Italy and Germany.

***Romanian money is called the leu. Just as cents make up the U.S. dollar, the leu is made up of* bani.**

Romanians have many different jobs. Some work in offices, banks, and restaurants. Others work in factories. They make things to sell to other countries, such as cars, clothing, and electronics. Romanian farmers grow wheat, corn, barley, and potatoes. They also raise chickens and sheep.

Many people visit Romania each year as tourists. They come to see the **medieval** castles and fortresses and enjoy the different landscapes.

**FACT!**

*Automobile Dacia, a car company, is one of Romania's largest and most successful businesses.*

***Bran Castle is just one of Romania's many castles. It is called Dracula's Castle but has little to do with the Dracula story.***

## LOOKING FOR DRACULA

Romania has a central region, or area, called Transylvania. The book *Dracula* said the main character, a vampire, came from there. Some tourists come to Romania because of this.

# THE ENVIRONMENT

Romania has many protected areas of nature, which are set aside and kept safe from building and other human activities. Close to one-fourth of the country is protected as national parks or other special areas.

The place where the Danube River meets the Black Sea is called the Danube Delta. It is the biggest marsh, or wetland, in Europe. Birds such as Dalmatian pelicans and ferruginous ducks lay eggs there in the summer. There are many species, or kinds, of fish such as pike, carp, and catfish too. Floating reeds and water lilies grow in the water.

Air and water pollution from factories is a problem in Romania. Also, parts of the Danube have been drained for farming. Today, Romania is trying harder to protect the **environment**.

### DANUBE DELTA NUMBERS

The Danube Delta is home to more than 370 bird species and 100 fish species. Several rare mammals live there too, such as the European otter.

The Danube is considered one of the most important waterway and fish **migration** paths of Europe. It also provides drinking water.

**FACT!**

Romania's national bird is the great white pelican, which lives in the Danube Delta.

In recent years, Romania has been changing to power sources that are better for the environment.

# THE PEOPLE TODAY

More than 19 million people call Romania home. About 90 percent are ethnically Romanian, or related to the Romans who lived there long ago. However, people with **ancestors** from other countries also live there, including Hungarians, Germans, Ukrainians, and others.

Romanians are friendly, welcoming people.

## THE COUNTRY LIFE

Nearly half of Romania's population lives in the countryside. Some Romanians are choosing to leave the cities for rural life. This is much different than most of Europe, where more people live in cities.

The Roma make up about 3 percent of the official population. They are also called Romani. The Roma came from South Asia a long time ago. Today, they live all over Europe. It is difficult to know how many Roma live in Romania because some are nomadic. This means that they move from place to place. Some do not report they are Roma because others look down on them and their culture.

**FACT!**
*Many Ukrainians moved to Romania after the start of the Russia-Ukraine War in 2022.*

*Many Roma people in Romania now stay in one place but may still practice their long-held traditions.*

# LIFESTYLE

Life for Romanians in rural, or countryside, areas is usually more traditional. Rural Romanians often have larger families with more family, such as grandparents, living in the same house. This does not happen often in the city. Instead, families are small, with only one or two children.

*Many families in rural Romania grow their own food and make things they need.*

## LIFE IN THE BIGGEST CITY

Bucharest offers trains and buses to get around. It also has a lot of big parks. People enjoy its restaurants and cultural activities, such as music and plays.

The Romanian constitution protects women's rights. At home and at work, women have the same rights as men. For example, women must be paid the same as men to do the same work.

All children must go to school through the tenth grade. High school continues through twelfth grade. Many students go to college. New laws were passed in 2023 to make the school system more successful for Romanian children.

**FACT!**

*Babeș-Bolyai University is the largest Romanian university, with about 50,000 students.*

As of 2023, Romanian children as young as four years old must begin school.

# RELIGION

Romania has no official religion. However, about three-fourths of all Romanians belong to the Romanian Orthodox Church. This is a kind of Christian church with a leader called a patriarch who is based in Bucharest. There are smaller groups of Romanians who are Roman Catholics and Protestants.

**FACT!**

*Religious leaders in Romania are partly paid by the government.*

*Around 17 million people practice the Romanian Orthodox religion. Shown is the National Cathedral in Bucharest.*

Before World War II, more than 700,000 Jewish people lived in Romania. During the war, many were killed or forced to move. Today, there are just a few thousand, who mostly live in or near Bucharest. In addition, about 76,000 Romanians are Muslim, which means they follow the religion of Islam. They mostly live near the Black Sea coast.

## RELIGIOUS PEOPLE

Less than one percent of Romanians do not follow a religion. Romania is one of the most religious countries in Europe.

*The Merry Cemetery in northern Romania is famous for its colorful tombstones and the sometimes funny sayings on them.*

# LANGUAGE

The official language of Romania is Romanian. About 90 percent of the people speak Romanian. Romanian is also spoken in Moldova, the country that borders Romania to the east. The Romanian language is used in schools, by the government, and for business.

Other languages are also spoken in Romania. About one million people speak Hungarian. People also speak Ukrainian, German, Serbian, Slovak, Russian, and Turkish.

**FACT!**
The Romanian language has its own holiday, Romanian Language Day, on August 31.

*This sign for a daycare program is written in Romanian and Hungarian. In some places, Hungarian is considered a co-official language.*

*The Romanian alphabet is like English. However, there are more letters, which have special markings.*

When Romania was communist, many of these languages were not allowed. For example, the Roma were not allowed to speak their language, called Romany. After Romania became democratic, people could speak their own languages again. Now, other languages are respected and even protected.

## ADDING TO THE ALPHABET

The Romanian alphabet is based on the Latin alphabet but has five more letters: Ă, Â, Î, Ș, Ț. The letters K, Q, W, and Y were not part of the official Romanian alphabet until 1982.

# ARTS AND FESTIVALS

In Romania, modern music has not erased a love of older, traditional folk music. Most folk music is played on the violin. Flutes or pipes can also be used, along with drums. Religious songs and special wedding songs are also performed with these instruments. Romania is known for the George Enescu classical music festival in Bucharest and the Untold electronic music festival in Cluj-Napoca.

**FACT!**
The town of Sighișoara hosts a festival celebrating its beginnings in medieval times.

The National Easter Egg Festival shows off Romania's tradition of decorating Easter eggs.

The Sibiu National Theater Festival is a large, 10-day performing arts celebration. People come from all over the world for classes, talks, and performances.

People perform folk dances along with folk music. These dances are usually performed in the countryside and during festivals. Often, the men of each community have a special dance. The dancing was once a way to show off in front of women they wanted to marry. There are also couples' dances and dances in which men jump over sticks.

## ZAMFIR

Some folk music artists have become famous worldwide. Gheorghe Zamfir is called the "master of the pan flute," a traditional Romanian instrument. His music appears in many hit movies.

# FUN AND PLAY

The most popular sport in Romania is soccer. It is called *fotbal* there. Both kids and adults love to play it. Thousands of people watch soccer clubs or the national soccer team play. The most popular soccer club is Steaua București in Bucharest.

Handball is another popular sport. Players pass a ball with their hands and try to get the ball in a goal. Other top sports to play and watch are volleyball, basketball, and tennis. Rowing sports are also very common.

As of 2026, Romania has won 22 Olympic gold medals for rowing and 10 gold medals for canoeing. Gymnastics is Romania's most successful Olympic sport with 24 gold medals and 73 in all.

### FAMOUS ROMANIAN

Nadia Comaneci is a famous Romanian gymnast who won many medals. In 1976, she became the first gymnast to score a perfect 10.0 at the Olympics.

People come from around the world to ski in the Carpathian Mountains.

**FACT!**

Oina is a traditional Romanian game that is a bit like baseball.

Romanian former professional handballer Cristina Neagu is often said to be the best player in the world.

# FOOD

Romanian food often uses the fruits and vegetables that are in season. Many dishes were **influenced** by the cultures that have called Romania home over time.

*Mămăligă* (muh-muh-LEE-guh) is a famous food that is made from cornmeal. Sometimes it is soft, like oatmeal. It can also be made more solid, so that it can be sliced like a bread. *Sarmale* is meat, often pork, mixed with rice and herbs and wrapped in cabbage leaves.

**FACT!**

*Mici is spiced meat, often pork, grilled up at Romanian street markets and fairs.*

*Sarmale is sometimes said to be the national dish of Romania. It is shown here with mămăligă and sour cream.*

Romania is also known for *ciorbă* (CHOR-buh), which are soups with a sour taste. They get their sourness from lemon juice, vinegar, or **sauerkraut** juice.

On the sweeter side are many desserts, such as the chocolate Joffre cake and *plăcintă* (plah-CHEEN-tah), a pastry filled with apples or sweet cheese. There's something for every taste on the Romanian table!

*Papanași (PAH-pah-nash) are Romanian donuts made from a soft cheese dough.*

## HOLIDAY EATING

Some foods are eaten on or around special days in Romania. For example, *tocaniță* is a meat and potato stew eaten around Christmas.

# GLOSSARY

**ancestor:** A relative who lived long before you.

**communist:** Having to do with a political and economic system where all property is shared by all the people.

**culture:** The beliefs and ways of life of a group of people.

**delta:** Land shaped like a triangle at the mouth of a river.

**economy:** The buying and selling of goods with money in a country.

**environment:** The natural world in which a plant or animal lives.

**influence:** To have an effect on.

**invade:** To enter a place to take it over.

**landscape:** An area of land with a certain appearance.

**medieval:** Having to do with the Middle Ages, a time in European history from about 500 to 1500.

**migration:** Movement to warmer or colder places for a season.

**prime minister:** The head of a government in some countries.

**revolution:** A movement to overthrow an established government.

**sauerkraut:** A German food made from small bits of cabbage soaked in a salty and sour liquid.

# FIND OUT MORE

## Books

Hansen, Grace. *Bran Castle*. Minneapolis, MN: Abdo Kids, 2022.

Spanier, Kristine. *Romania*. Minneapolis, MN: Pogo, 2023.

## Websites

**Romania**
*kids.britannica.com/kids/article/Romania/345772*
Read an overview of this interesting country on the Britannica Kids website.

**Where in the World? Romania**
*www.funkidslive.com/learn/where-the-world/romania/*
Find out how to say "hello" in Romanian and more on this fun site.

## Video

**Gheorghe Zamfir**
*www.youtube.com/watch?v=xY4vVerjtHU*
Watch the famous pan flute player perform his most beloved song in Romania.

**Publisher's note to educators and parents:** Our editors have carefully reviewed these websites to ensure that they are suitable for students. Many websites change frequently, however, and we cannot guarantee that a site's future contents will continue to meet our high standards of quality and educational value. Be advised that students should be closely supervised whenever they access the internet.

# INDEX